my itty-bitty bio

John Muir

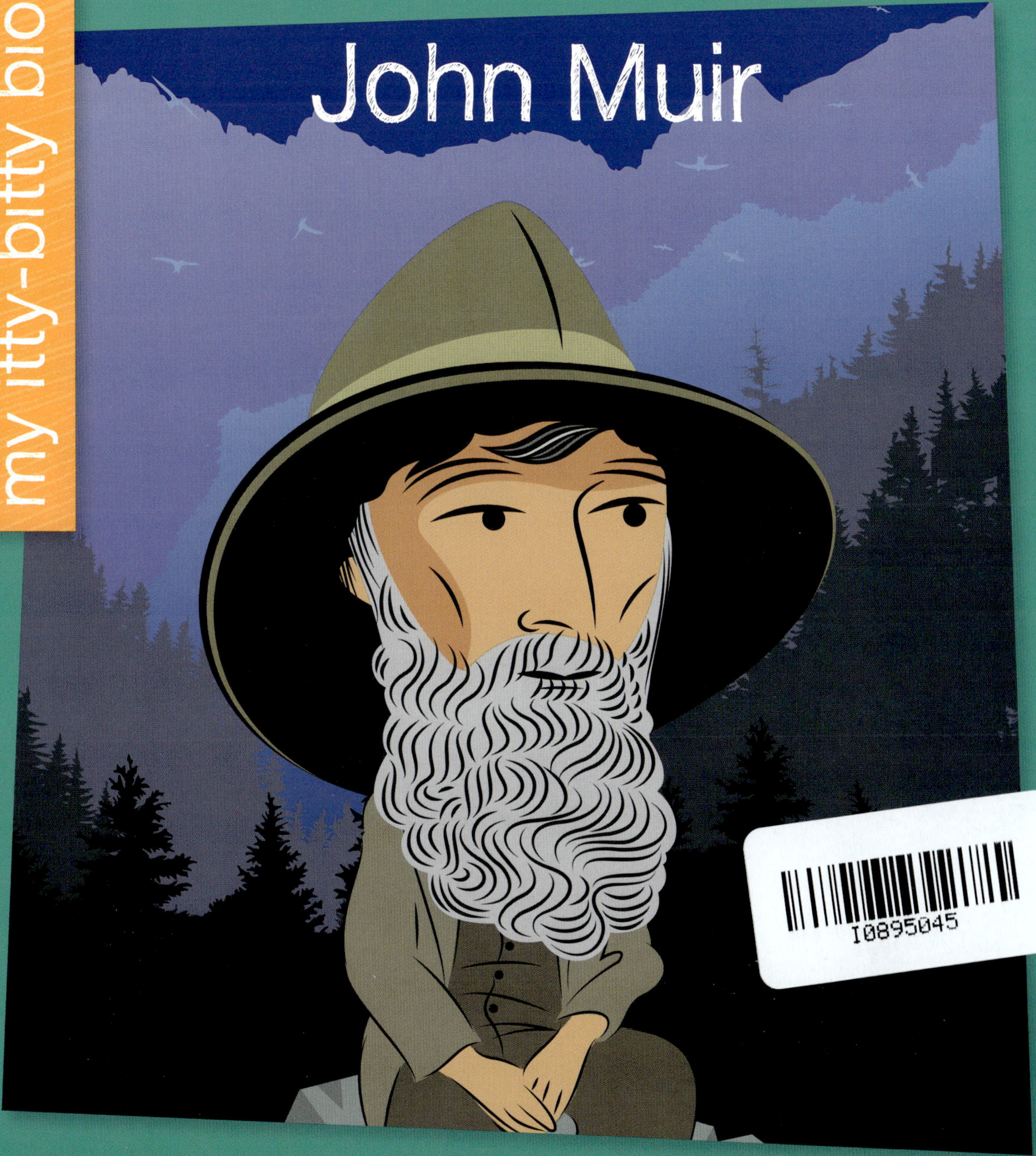

Published in the United States of America by Cherry Lake Publishing
Ann Arbor, Michigan
www.cherrylakepublishing.com

Content Adviser: Ryan Emery Hughes, Doctoral Student, School of Education, University of Michigan
Reading Adviser: Marla Conn MS, Ed., Literacy specialist, Read-Ability, Inc.
Book Design: Jennifer Wahl
Illustrator: Jeff Bane

Photo Credits: © digitalreflections / Shutterstock.com, 5; © Tom Grundy / Shutterstock.com, 7; © Zack Frank / Shutterstock.com, 9, 22; © Jason Mintzer / Shutterstock.com, 11; © Boris15 / Shutterstock.com, 13; © Everett Historical / Shutterstock.com, 15; © Tobin Akehurst / Shutterstock.com, 17, 23; © Radoslaw Lecyk / Shutterstock.com, 19; © Harmony Gerber / Shutterstock.com, 21; Cover, 1, 6, 10, 12, Jeff Bane; Various frames throughout, Shutterstock.com

Library of Congress Cataloging-in-Publication Data

Names: Devera, Czeena, author.
Title: John Muir / Czeena Devera.
Description: Ann Arbor, MI : Cherry Lake Publishing, [2017] | Series: My itty-bitty bio | Audience: K to grade 3.
Identifiers: LCCN 2016056238| ISBN 9781634728140 (hardcover) | ISBN 9781634729925 (pbk.) | ISBN 9781634729031 (pdf) | ISBN 9781534100817 (ebook)
Subjects: LCSH: Muir, John, 1838-1914--Juvenile literature. | Naturalists--United States--Biography--Juvenile literature. | Conservationists--United States--Biography--Juvenile literature.
Classification: LCC QH31.M9 D48 2017 | DDC 333.7/2/092 [B] --dc23
LC record available at https://lccn.loc.gov/2016056238

Printed in the United States of America
Corporate Graphics

table of contents

About the author: Czeena Devera grew up in the sweltering heat of Arizona surrounded by books, quite literally as her childhood bedroom had built-in bookshelves constantly overflowing. She now lives in Michigan with an even bigger library of books.

About the illustrator: Jeff Bane and his two business partners own a studio along the American River in Folsom, California, home of the 1849 Gold Rush. When Jeff's not sketching or illustrating for clients, he's either swimming or kayaking in the river to relax.

I was born in Scotland. It was 1838.

My family moved to the United States.

I went to college. I did not finish.

I traveled a lot.

Where would you like to travel?

I moved to California. I got married.

We had two daughters. I loved my family.

I also loved nature. I saw forests being destroyed.

I wanted to save the trees.

I visited Yosemite. It was a wild area in California.

I helped it become a **national park**.

I **published** books.

President Theodore Roosevelt read one. He liked it. We worked together.

I helped start the Sierra Club.

This club keeps nature safe.

My state needed water. They took water from Yosemite.

This upset me.

What makes you unhappy?
How can you fix it?

I died in 1914. I am the father of our national park system.

National parks are still important today. My love of nature lives on.

What would you like to ask me?

timeline

1880

1820

Born

1838

1892

1920

Died
1914

glossary & index

glossary

national park (NASH-uh-nuhl PAHRK) a large section of land that is kept safe by the government and that people can visit

published (PUHB-lishd) produced a book that many people can read

index